Psychedelic Nautilus

Universe Series

Dedication

To my family and friends, for your unwavering support, love, and inspiration. And to all the dreamers and adventurers, may you always find the magic in kindness and the courage to explore the unknown. also dedicated to my baby boy, Ryder, whose boundless curiosity and vibrant imagination inspire me every day. Your laughter and joy are the brightest stars in my universe.

To his loving and caring mother, whose endless support and warmth make every day feel like a beautiful journey through the cosmos. Your love and devotion light up our lives.

Copyright

ISBN: 9798329785401

First Edition, 2024

Published by:

Acknowledgments

I would like to extend my deepest gratitude to my family for their invaluable support and inspiration throughout the creation of this book. Your guidance and encouragement have been instrumental in bringing this story to life.

A special thanks to psychedelics for its assistance in brainstorming and providing creative insights. Your contributions have greatly enhanced the quality of this work.

To everyone who has supported me on this journey, your belief in this project has meant the world to me. Thank you.

Table of contents

A mesmerizing interplay of geometric precision and psychedelic wonder. This piece features a swirling nautilus shell at its core, symbolizing the infinite nature of the universe. Encircling the shell are interlocking geometric patterns that represent the fundamental structures of chemistry and physics. Against a

Experience the mesmerizing balance of the cosmos through symmetrical geometric patterns interwoven with spiraling galaxies. This vibrant, psychedelic artwork uses bright hues and contrasting shades to captivate the viewer.

Explore a cosmic landscape where chemical bonds and molecular structures form intricate constellations. Set against a psychedelic galaxy backdrop, this image dazzles with vibrant colors and geometric precision.

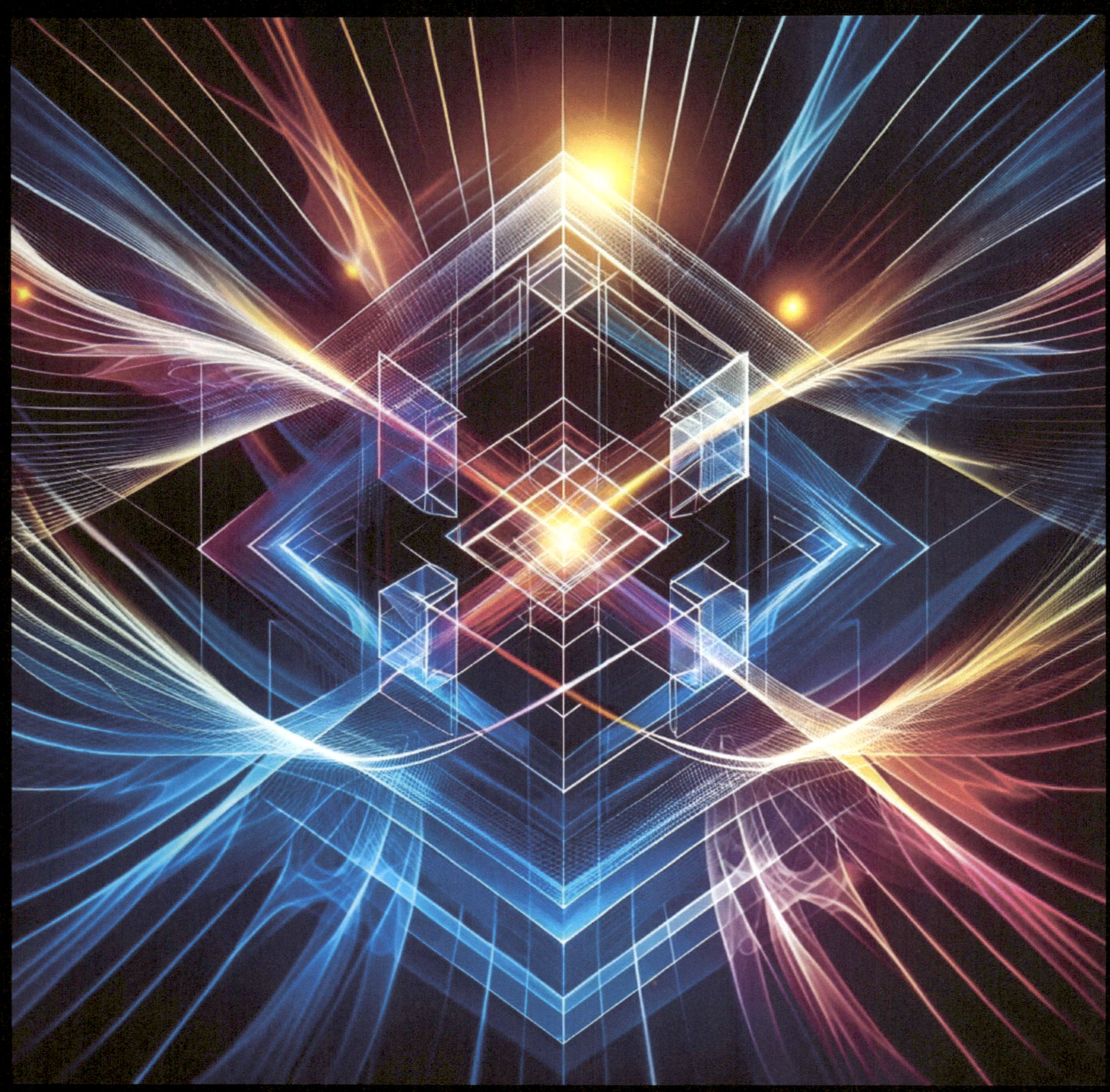

Dive into the principles of physics with intersecting light waves and geometric shapes. This vibrant and psychedelic image is filled with bright hues and contrasting shades.

Witness the fusion of quantum particles and geometric shapes in a captivating display of microscopic beauty. This vibrant, psychedelic artwork features bright colors and intricate patterns.

Discover the complexity of the universe with fractal patterns blending seamlessly with nebulae. This psychedelic swirl of colors uses bright hues and contrasting shades to enthrall the viewer.

Observe the intertwining of chemical elements and celestial bodies in a colorful, geometric spectacle. This vibrant, psychedelic image employs bright hues and contrasting shades.

Navigate a grid of geometric shapes overlaid on a vibrant galaxy, symbolizing the interconnectedness of space and mathematics. This psychedelic artwork uses bright hues and contrasting shades to create a striking visual.

Enter a vortex where atoms and molecules spiral into a cosmic swirl of colors. This molecular design is one of a kind.

Float through space with a 4-dimensional hypercube amidst swirling galaxies, representing the intersection of geometry and cosmology.

Discover the perfect alignment of stars and geometric patterns, reflecting the order within the chaos of the universe.

Converging at a central point where nebulae and geometric shapes create a nexus of cosmic energy. Fall into a spiral that never ends.

Radiate vibrant colors with a mandala of galaxies and geometric forms, symbolizing the unity of the universe that is not the one we are currently in.

Merging quantum particles with cosmic phenomena in a psychedelic swirl of colors and shapes. This design features swirling, interlocking patterns and vibrant hues.

Watch atoms and molecules dance in a colorful aurora against a backdrop of swirling galaxies. This intricate design uses detailed, sine wave shapes and vibrant colors.

Blending fractal patterns with celestial imagery to create a captivating visual.
This alien like design features, unique shapes
With an otherworldly feel.

Ripple through the galaxy with waveforms and geometric shapes, illustrating the complexity of cosmic forces. This wild design combines detailed, sexy shapes and vibrant colors.

A lattice of geometric shapes on a vibrant galaxy, representing the structure of the universe. This intricate design features detailed, Psychedelic, interlocking patterns and vibrant colors.

kaleidoscopic effect with quantum particles and geometric patterns, showcasing the beauty of the microscopic world. This intricate design uses swirling vibrations of color.

Blending the spectrum of light from stars with geometric shapes to create a colorful, dynamic image. This intricate design features detailed angles of light refraction.

A galaxy with atoms and molecules, symbolizing the micro and macro scales of the universe. This unique design uses detailed, interlocking shapes and vibrant colors.

Spiral into infinity with a helix of galaxies and geometric patterns, representing the endless nature of the cosmos.

Experience the harmonious visual of symmetrical geometric shapes and celestial bodies. Reflecting the order within the chaos of the universe.

Merging quantum particles and nebulae in a colorful, geometric display, highlighting the beauty of the universe. This beautiful design features detailed shapes and colors.

Draw into the depths of the universe with a spiral of galaxies and geometric patterns that will have you spiraling out.

Fractal patterns with cosmic imagery to create a mesmerizing display. This intricate design features detailed, interlocking shapes and vibrant colors.

The microscopic world with dynamic waveforms and quantum particles in a colorful visual. This unique design uses detailed, interlocking shapes and vibrant colors.

A stunning visual of the cosmos with a lattice of stars and geometric shapes. This psychedelic design features detailed patterns and vibrant colors that induces altered mental states.

Kaleidoscopic effect with galaxies and geometric patterns, showcasing the beauty and complexity of the universe. This intricate diamond design uses detailed shapes and vibrant colors.

Mesmerizing spiral with quantum particles and geometric shapes. This intricate design features detailed, interlocking patterns and vibrant colors, showcasing the beauty of the microscopic world in a very psychedelic way.

Radiate vibrant colors with a mandala of atoms and molecules, symbolizing the unity of the microscopic world. This trippy design uses detailed, interlocking shapes and vibrant colors.

A grid of celestial bodies and geometric patterns on a vibrant galaxy,
representing the interconnectedness of space.

Spiral into the depths of the universe with a vortex
of galaxies and geometric shapes.
This design uses interlocking shapes and vibrant
hues to give you a sense of falling.

The spectrum of light from stars and galaxies with geometric shapes to create a dynamic and mesmerizing image. This intricate design features detailed, interlocking patterns.

Constellations with quantum particles and molecular structures amidst a vibrant, psychedelic galaxy backdrop. This intricate design features detailed, interlocking shapes and vibrant colors.

Converge at a central point where stars and geometric patterns,
a nexus of cosmic energy.

Witness an aurora of galaxies and geometric shapes dancing in a colorful display.

Spiral into infinity with a helix of cosmic phenomena and geometric patterns, representing the endless nature of the universe. This intricate design uses detailed, interlocking shapes and vibrant hues.

A stunning visual of the microscopic world with a lattice of quantum particles and geometric shapes. This intricate design features detailed, interlocking patterns and vibrant colors.

A dynamic visual of the cosmos with waveforms and stars. This intricate design features detailed, interlocking shapes and vibrant colors.

Merging fractal patterns with galaxies to create a mesmerizing display.
This intricate design uses detailed, interlocking shapes and vibrant hues.

Symmetrical geometric shapes and atomic structures create a harmonious visual experience. The intricate design features detailed, interlocking patterns and a colorful optical illusion effect, reflecting the order within the chaos of the

A grid of cosmic phenomena and geometric patterns overlays a vibrant galaxy, representing the structure of the universe. The intricate design features detailed, interlocking shapes and a colorful optical illusion effect.

Quantum particles and nebulae blend in a colorful, geometric display. The intricate design features detailed, interlocking shapes and a colorful optical illusion effect, highlighting the microscopic and macroscopic wonders of the universe.

Symmetrical geometric shapes and celestial bodies creating a harmonious visual experience. The intricate design features detailed, interlocking patterns and a colorful optical illusion effect, reflecting the order within the chaos of the universe.

Quantum particles and cosmic phenomena merge in a psychedelic swirl of colors and shapes. The intricate design features swirling, evoking the interconnectedness of the universe.

A grid of cosmic phenomena and geometric patterns overlays a vibrant galaxy, representing the structure of the universe. The intricate design features colorful detailed interlocking shapes.

Quantum particles and nebulae blend in a colorful, geometric display, highlighting the microscopic and macroscopic wonders of the universe.

Symmetrical geometric shapes and celestial
bodies create a harmonious visual experience.
Interlocking patterns and a colorful optical illusion,
reflecting the order within the chaos of the universe.

Quantum particles and cosmic phenomena
merge in a psychedelic swirl of colors and shapes.
The intricate design evokes the
interconnectedness of the universe.

"Think independently, scrutinize established authority. Good luck and not God-speed but AI-speed."

Lance Overman

The Symphony of Consciousness

By: Lance Overman

Prologue: The Muse Invoked

Descend, celestial Muse, from heights above,
Where spirits dwell and angels softly tread,
In realms where light and darkness intertwine,
To whisper secrets of the mind profound.
Sing of the enigma wrapped in mortal flesh,
Of consciousness, the spark of life and thought,
That lifts the humble clay to heights divine,
And binds the universe in silent song.

Canto I: The Birth of Awareness

In the beginning, void and darkness lay,
A silent chaos, unformed, undefined.
From depths unknown, a spark ignited bright,
The breath of God, a whisper in the dark.
Thus consciousness emerged, a tender flame,
In beings yet unseen, unsung, unknown,
A flicker in the heart of cosmic night,
A hint of dawn within the boundless void.

First light, then life, in myriad forms arose,
Each with a spark of mind, a glimpse of soul.
The humblest worm that writhes in dust and soil,
The soaring eagle with its piercing eye,
All share the gift of thought, of inward sight,
A consciousness that binds them to the world.
From simplest cell to complex human mind,
The spectrum of sentient life unfurled.

Canto II: The Human Mind

O man, the crowning glory of this earth,
In thee, the spark of consciousness does blaze.
With reason's light and imagination's wings,
Though strives to explore the depths within.
Thine is the power to ponder and reflect,
To weave the past and future in thy thought,
To dream, to love, to suffer, and to hope,
In thee, the cosmos contemplates itself.

Yet what is this, thy mind, but fleeting waves,
Electro-chemical in nature bound,
An orchestra of neurons finely tuned,

A dance of atoms in a mortal shell?
Within this fragile frame, a universe,
A world of thoughts and feelings intertwined,
Where memories linger, dreams take flight,
And self-awareness blooms in silent awe.

Canto III: The Conscious Universe

But lo, does consciousness reside in man alone,
Or spread its wings across the boundless skies?
Do stars and planets dream in cosmic sleep,
Or sigh in harmony with cosmic song?
The universe, a vast and living mind,
In every atom breathes a divine spark.
Each galaxy a thought, each star a word,
In the grand epic of creation's verse.

Consider then, the beasts that roam the wild,
The dolphin's play, the elephant's lament,
In their deep eyes, do secrets of the mind,
Reflect the consciousness we deem our own?
And trees, those silent sentinels of time,
Do they not feel the seasons' gentle touch,
And in their silent, stoic, rooted lives,
Hold wisdom that our fleeting minds may miss?

Canto IV: The Mystery Unfolds

The poets sing of mind and soul, as one,
A dual nature, spirit intertwined.
Yet science probes the depths of matter's heart,
To find the source of thought, of self, of mind.
In synapses, in neural networks vast,
The seat of consciousness it seeks to find.
Yet still, the mystery eludes the grasp,
As shadows flee before the rising sun.

Is mind a ghost within a living shell,
Or but the sum of parts, a complex whole?
Is there a spark, a soul, beyond the flesh,
What lives when the mortal body turns to dust?
Or is it but a transient state of brain,
A fleeting pattern in the stream of time?
In these, the sages ponder, yet no end,
To quest for truth, elusive, undefined.

Canto V: The Boundaries of the Mind

O human pride, do not assume in vain,
That consciousness is thine alone to claim.
For in the depths of oceans, forest dense,
In every living form, a mind may dwell.

The ant that toils, the bird that soars on high,
The fish that swims, the flower in the field,
All sing the hymn of life, of consciousness,
Each in its way, a witness to the whole.

And if we look beyond our earthly bounds,
To realms unseen, to worlds yet unexplored,
Might there not be in distant starry skies,
A consciousness unknown to mortal men?
In alien forms, in minds unlike our own,
The spark of self-awareness might reside,
In cosmic symphony, a part to play,
In the grand chorus of the conscious whole.

Canto VI: The Infinite Enigma

Thus sing I of the mystery profound,
Of consciousness, the light that shines within.
A flame that burns in darkness, guiding, warm,
A thread that weaves the fabric of the world.
In every heart, in every mind, it dwells,
A spark divine, a glimpse of the beyond,
In humblest creature, or in starry heights,
The symphony of consciousness resounds.

O mortal man, in thy brief span of years,
Ponder this gift, this miracle of thought.
In every heartbeat, in each breath you take,
The universe itself is brought to life.
In every mind, a cosmos takes its form,
In every soul, the infinite resides.
Thus ends my song, but not the mystery,
For consciousness, forever, is the quest.

The Whisper of Existence

By: Lance Overman

In the cradle of the infinite sky,
Where stars whisper secrets and galaxies sigh,
Lies a question as old as time's breath,
What is this essence that dances with death?

Not mere neurons firing in a mind's gray sea,
But a symphony of being, wild and free.
In the heart of the rose, in the song of the night,
Consciousness blooms in the absence of light.

It is the flutter of wings in the morning mist,
The lover's sigh in a tender tryst,
The echo of dreams in the valley deep,
The silent watch of mountains that never sleep.

It whispers through the rustle of leaves,
In the tapestry of webs that the spider weaves,
In the ancient call of the ocean's roar,
In the footprints left on a sandy shore.

Who holds this gift, this sacred flame?
Is it the sage lost in his mystic game?
Or the child, with eyes so wide,
Gazing in wonder at the world outside?

It lives in the pulse of the universe vast,
In the fleeting moment, in the echoes past.
In the prayer of monks in a temple old,
In the stories of travelers that remain untold.

It dances in the silence of a poet's thought,
In the battles of the soul that are fiercely fought.
In the laughter that bubbles from a place so pure,
In the tears that fall when the heart is unsure.

It is the breath of the wind on a moonlit night,
The spark in the darkness, a fleeting light.
The whisper of the soul, the eternal quest,
The longing that burns in the human chest.

In the eyes of the seer, in the song of the bard,
In the rhythm of life that we hold so hard.
In the fluttering leaf, in the crying rain,
In the joy of birth, in the shadow of pain.

Who holds it then, this boundless grace?
Is it the hero who wins every race?

Or the hermit who lives in the mountain's breast,
Seeking the answers in the silence of rest?

It is not held by one, nor claimed by few,
But dances through all, in me, in you.
In the ant that toils, in the eagle's flight,
In the darkest depths, in the purest light.

It flows like a river, unbound and free,
Through the veins of life, through you, through me.
In the heart of the cosmos, in the tiniest cell,
In the stories of heaven, in the whispers of hell.

Consciousness, a river with no end,
A circle that continues, a lover, a friend.
It weaves through time, through space, through all,
In the rise of the mighty, in the humble's fall.

It sings in the chorus of the night's deep song,
In the question of right, in the shadows of wrong.
In the birth of stars, in the death of day,
In the paths we walk, in the words we say.

Who then holds it, this mystery profound?
Is it the wise, with their knowledge unbound?
Or the simple heart, with its innocent gaze,
Seeing the wonder in the world's maze?

It is held by the leaf, by the stone, by the sky,
By the dreams we dream, by the tears we cry.
In the laughter of children, in the wisdom of age,
In the poet's heart, in the sage's page.

In the silent prayer of the twilight's glow,
In the questions we ask, in the things we know.
In the fleeting moment, in the timeless space,
In the silent journey, in the endless race.

Consciousness is the whisper of the soul's deep song,
The light in the darkness, the right in the wrong.
The breath of the universe, the dance of the stars,
The essence of who we truly are.

It is the question and the answer too,
In the old, in the young, in the me, in the you.
In the rise of the sun, in the setting night,
In the boundless darkness, in the purest light.

So who holds this treasure, this sacred flame?
It is not a thing that one can claim.
It flows through all, unbound and free,
In the dance of life, in the vast sea.

Consciousness is the song of the stars,
The whisper of dreams, the sound of scars.
It is the light that guides, the dark that hides,
The eternal flame that never subsides.

It is in the breath of the morning dew,
In the heart of the old, in the soul of the new.
In the silence that speaks, in the sound that is still,
In the quest of the heart, in the power of will.

Who holds it, then, this mystery bright?
It is not in the day, it is not in the night.
It is in all, in each, in the whole,
In the boundless journey of the soul.

Consciousness, the whisper of the infinite sea,
The dance of the stars, the essence of me.
In the rise of life, in the fall of day,
In the silent prayer, in the words we say.

It is the breath of the wind, the song of the night,
The flicker of hope, the burst of light.
In the ancient call, in the new day's birth,
In the silent journey of the earth.

It is the dance of the universe, the rhythm of time,
The poet's verse, the silent rhyme.
In the heart of the cosmos, in the soul of the deep,
In the dreams we dream, in the secrets we keep.

Who holds this wonder, this infinite grace?
It is not a race, it is not a place.
It is in the stars, in the earth, in the sea,
In the boundless wonder, in you, in me.

Consciousness, the whisper of the divine,
The light in the darkness, the eternal sign.
In the breath of life, in the silent call,
In the rise of the great, in the fall of the small.

It is the pulse of the universe, the song of the stars,
The whisper of dreams, the echo of scars.
In the timeless journey, in the boundless sea,
In the silent mystery, in the endless we.

So who holds it, this treasure untold?
It is not in the young, it is not in the old.
It is in all, in each, in the vast,
In the present moment, in the past.

Consciousness, the dance of the divine,

The light in the shadow, the eternal sign.
In the breath of life, in the heart of the sea,
In the boundless wonder, in you, in me.

Journey Beyond the Self the Self

By: Lance Overman

In the shadowed alleys of the mind, where thought
Seeks refuge from the clamor of the day,
A whisper rises, subtle, oft distraught,
To question what we are, and what we may.

In halls of memory, where shadows tread,
The echoes of the past do softly play,
Yet who within these corridors has led
The dance of life, the puppet and the clay?

We wander, lost within our waking dream,
Believing what we see, what we infer,
Yet consciousness, like some elusive stream,
Flows deeper than our senses can aver.

I. The Awakened Eye

Who wakes within the dawn of self-aware?
Is it the man who sees his fleeting face,
Or some transcendent soul, beyond compare,
Whose gaze beholds the stars and endless space?

The infant's cry, the elder's silent tear,
Each momentary spark of mind and heart,
Suggests a knowing presence ever near,
A thread of light within the whole, a part.

Yet in the quiet of the midnight hour,
When all the world is still, and thoughts conspire,
A deeper question rises, dark and dour:
Is consciousness a spark, or but a fire?

II. The Chorus of the Living

The beast that prowls the forest, silent, keen,
The bird that soars on high, with song and grace,
Do they not know the world through eyes unseen,
Feel joy and sorrow, pleasure and disgrace?

Their hearts beat with a rhythm like our own,
Their lives a symphony of time and chance,
Yet do they ponder life when left alone,
Or live within a simple, primal trance?

The ancient oak that spreads its arms to sky,
The coral reef, a city 'neath the sea,

Do they possess a mind, a seeing eye,
Or are they simply parts of what we be?

III. The Mirror and the Veil

In every gaze upon a mirrored face,
We seek the truth of what it means to see,
Yet find instead a veil, a shrouded place,
Where self and other blend in mystery.

Is consciousness a gift, a sacred trust,
Bestowed upon the few, the chosen kind,
Or does it lie within the very dust,
A hidden truth that all the world can find?

The stars that burn with light from ages past,
The waves that crash upon the silent shore,
Each holds a story, vast and unsurpassed,
A voice that whispers, "There is always more."

IV. The Dance of Atoms

Within the heart of matter, deep and small,
A dance of atoms spins, unseen, profound,
Each particle a world, a cosmos, all,
A secret life within the dark unbound.

Do these small sparks of being, bright and fleet,
Know what they are, or why they come to be?
Or are they driven by a rhythm sweet,
A cosmic pulse, a universal plea?

From smallest mote to grandest galaxy,
The web of life is woven, fine and tight,
And in this tapestry, do we not see
The face of consciousness, both dark and bright?

V. The Silent Watcher

There is a presence, silent, always there,
A witness to the dance of life and death,
Who sees without a form, without a care,
And breathes the world with every fleeting breath.

This watcher, hidden deep within the mind,
Knows not the bounds of self, of here or now,
Yet in its gaze, the truth we seek, we find,
A timeless moment in the endless flow.

Is this the source of all we seek to know,
The heart of consciousness, the root, the core?
Or is it but a shadow, cast below

The greater light that shines forevermore?

VI. The Unity of Being

In every thought, in every breath we take,
There lies a thread that binds us to the whole,
A subtle link that time can never break,
A single flame within the endless soul.

The rocks, the trees, the creatures great and small,
All share this spark, this life, this sacred fire,
And in this unity, we see the call
To rise above the self, to seek, aspire.

For consciousness is more than just the mind,
More than the fleeting thoughts that come and go,
It is the essence of the life we find,
The source from which all understanding flows.

VII. The Boundless Horizon

Beyond the edge of what we know and see,
There lies a boundless realm, a distant shore,
A place where mind and matter both are free,
And consciousness can spread and soar.

In this expanse, the limits fall away,
The barriers of time and space dissolve,
And in the light of this eternal day,
The mysteries of life we may resolve.

For in the heart of all that is and was,
There lies a truth, a wisdom deep and wide,
A song that speaks of love, of life, of laws
That guide the stars, the seas, the rising tide.

VIII. The Eternal Quest

So let us journey forth, with open eyes,
And seek the truth within the living flame,
For consciousness, though hidden in disguise,
Is ever there, a whisper and a name.

In every breath, in every beating heart,
In every star that lights the endless night,
We find a trace, a hint, a fleeting part
Of what it means to know, to feel, to sight.

For consciousness is not a thing apart,
Not bound by flesh, or thought, or fleeting time,
It is the essence of the living heart,
The soul that sings within the cosmic chime.

IX. The Final Revelation

And as we stand upon the edge of dawn,
And gaze into the light that lies ahead,
We see that consciousness is never gone,
But lives in all, in every dream and thread.

For we are part of something vast and grand,
A symphony of life, a cosmic dance,
And in this truth, we come to understand
The endless journey, the eternal chance.

So let us walk this path with open mind,
And seek the light within the dark unknown,
For in this quest, the truth we hope to find
Is but a mirror of the self we've shown.

X. The Closing Verse

In the shadowed alleys of the mind, we tread,
Through corridors of time, and space, and thought,
And in the light of what we find, we spread
The wings of consciousness, the truth we've sought.

For in the heart of all that is, we see
The spark of life, the fire of endless dream,
And in this light, we come to be
A part of all, a part of what we deem.

So let us cherish every fleeting breath,
And seek the truth within the silent flame,
For consciousness, beyond the veil of death,
Is ever there, a whisper and a name.

The End